Adam,

Always Remember...

You Are Worth It!

TAKING
THE WAR OUT OF THE
WARRIOR

An Inspirational Journey
Through Divorce & Healing
Into Empowerment, Self-Discovery & Spirituality

TJ MENHENNITT

BALBOA.
PRESS

A DIVISION OF HAY HOUSE

One quote from the bible is included in the Worthy Chapter ("I can do all things through Christ who strengthens me"). It was taken from biblegateway.com. In the footnotes on that quote on the website, it says it is from Philippians 4:13 from the New King James Version

Balboa Press books may be ordered through booksellers or by contacting:

Balboa Press
A Division of Hay House
1663 Liberty Drive
Bloomington, IN 47403
www.balboapress.com
1 (877) 407-4847

Print information available on the last page.

ISBN: 978-1-9822-2128-7 (sc)
ISBN: 978-1-9822-2130-0 (hc)
ISBN: 978-1-9822-2129-4 (e)

Library of Congress Control Number: 2019901311

Balboa Press rev. date: 02/12/2019

For my mom, Lois Ann, the woman who has always been my example of prayer and perseverance. To this day, she has practiced the importance of spiritual, physical, and mental exercise every day. My story would be very different without her. I love you Mom.

CONTENTS

INTRODUCTION

"Everything is held together with stories. That is all that is holding us together, stories and compassion."
~Barry Lopez

Before we dive into my journey, I would like to take the time to say thank you for picking up this book and giving my story a chance. Most likely, there is something going on in your life, and I'm truly sorry. I want you to know whatever pain or hurt you went through or are experiencing, there is hope and you are loved. You might not believe that or even understand it at this time, but you are worth it.

My trials of hurt were during the time when I was going through a separation with my wife. I believed that all of my emotional pain was brought on because of the fallout of my marriage. In the end, however, that chapter in my life was merely a door that opened unlocked hidden truths about myself. They were hard truths, as I will explain throughout this story, truths that I not only had to face but that also led to a choice to either remain and dwell in the past or to advance and open the next chapter of my life.

Every day is a day worth living. At one time, I didn't believe that. I didn't think anyone cared, nor did I believe I would survive. I was definitely at my worst. You might say I was at the bottom, and I really didn't see a way up and out. But today, I am able to look back in amazement. I went from "hell" to paradise... my paradise, my happiness. And this book captures that journey.

If you are going through a trying time in your life, or even if life is pretty good but you just wish you could experience more happiness, perhaps something from my journey can help. And if nothing else, I hope it will inspire you to never give up on yourself and to keep moving forward in growth. That is my wish.

CHAPTER ONE

Derailed

*"Where there is anger, there is always
pain underneath."*
~Eckhart Tolle

With my head in the sink and water running over my face, I lift my head and open my eyes. As the water drips down my face, I stare in the mirror and see a man I no longer recognize. The young man with dreams who once was full of happiness and peace no longer exists. Instead, I see the reflection of a bitter person who doesn't feel human anymore; he's robotic and soulless, not to mention overweight, tired, and stiff.

My bloodshot eyes can barely open, but they open enough to see the reflection of a lost person who is barely alive. Anger and pain have tired me and I'm not sure how much longer I can get up each day and pretend. It's an anger that has plagued my system and a pain that has entirely broken me.

As I stand there, I wonder if last night was a dream, those two little children of mine saving my life. As I continued to splash water over my face and stare in the mirror, I also wonder if the entire previous year was just a nightmare.

> *"It's easy to lose sight of the ultimate goal when you're in the trenches."*
> *~Tony Dungy*

You see, I was going through a separation, something I never dreamed could happen, and to put it lightly, it was something I wasn't handling well. Every day for over a year with sleepless nights and hate, I dug myself deeper and deeper into what I called *The Trenches*. Trench warfare was used in World War I. Enemies would dig long trenches that were deep enough to stand in to be out of the line of open fire, and sometimes they would live in the trenches for long periods of time without being seen by the opposing enemy. I had basically trenched myself from life as I previously knew it.

Each day, I would get up with zero rest and go off to work, and one thing's for sure, exhaustion will do some crazy things to you. First, it left me fatigued; second, it really messed with my mind. Paranoia sets in and makes you believe things are happening when they really aren't. Almost every time I would lay down to try to sleep, a little voice in my head would be there to tell me things that weren't true or make me believe things were all happening behind my back. As you read ahead, you'll learn that I did find a way to end all of that, but it took many long months of suffering, not only for me, but for my entire family. It's something I truly regret.

Anger and hate snuck their way in while I was in the trenches and it made for nice ammunition whenever needed. Conversations would always lead to arguments. I was mad at everyone and hated myself the worst. Because of this hate, fear made me trust no one, and that can be pretty lonely. Yes, for over a year, I lived like that, but for the most part, I hid as much of my pain from my children as I could. Whatever little strength I had left in me each day, I tried like hell to be there for them.

Day in and day out for over a year, this went on and then one night after work, I decided to go outside and light a fire in the firepit. I grabbed a bunch of beers and started drinking one after another. I stared into the fire, and started to relive every event in my life from my childhood to the present day, and I kept asking myself, "Where did I go wrong? Why is this happening to me?" I was asking lots of questions as I stared into that fire, but no answers were coming back.

That's when I started to feel one of the worst feelings a person can have, the feeling of being unworthy. I felt I wasn't worth anything anymore. Hate and anger fueled with every beer. I stared into that fire, and then it happened. I broke, and I started to cry. I was so tired and so alone at that moment, all I could do was cry.

I realized I was becoming a disgrace, not only to everyone around me, but also to myself. I was overweight, I had no strength, and my muscles were tensed and fatigued from fear. I lost track of being a father, and I was just going through the motions, trying to survive each day.

I remember thinking about my options. I knew that if I stayed on that path, I would either do myself in with a massive heart attack or a stroke (which I felt could really happen at any second), or I could just take the easy way out and do myself in. It's horrible to think about, but it was true and there were many days prior to that night when I had given it thought. That's what fear will do to you; once it goes into full mode, your thoughts can start to overtake your wellbeing and common sense.

Fear drove me to some horrible thoughts and as I went for another beer, and in full sob, two little heads came bursting outside to tell me that they were going to bed. I had no time to wipe the tears from my face, and they started to hug me and ask why I was crying. "Please stop crying Daddy, it will be okay," they said, even though they had no idea why I was crying. I felt their innocence in saying what we all tend to say: "It's going to be okay."

I could smell that they were freshly showered as I hugged them so tight. I needed that hug, and as I look back now, it was the start of many saving graces. I told them to hurry to bed and that I would be up to tuck them in. As they left in a flash, I stared back one more time at the fire, wiped the tears from my face, and I realized I had a third option: I could get up and try like hell to forge on. I had no idea how and I had no plan, but I had to try, and I remember saying out loud, "I need help."

I took the remaining beers and poured them into the fire, and then I went upstairs and tucked my two beautiful children into bed, letting them know how much I love them and telling them to sleep tight.

Like I said previously, there are many things that we truly miss when we live in fear, and we tend to believe things that really aren't true. It's like a cloud or a fog that overcomes you, similar to a hot, hazy, humid summer day when everything you look at has a mild blur to it.

We forget that someone, somewhere truly loves us. Maybe you don't have children to remind you of that, but you have someone. Take a minute or two and think over what love really means. If you aren't experiencing love in your life, it could be because you have none to share. This was truly my experience; I had no love inside of me. I hated myself so much that hate was the only thing I could see in the world. On that night, those two little children of mine reminded me that love was still alive and that I was worth something to them. And so are you. You are worth it. You are worth something to someone, and you are worth something to yourself.

"Don't give up before the miracle happens."
~Fannie Flagg

After tucking my kids into bed, I came downstairs to the sofa, and got myself ready for another restless night. I had started to accept the routine of not sleeping, getting up with a sore back, and heading off to work. But tonight was different; I was finally distracted from the constant worries of the unknown. Tonight, I didn't feel the tension of anger and hate. This time, I had a slight feeling of relief for the first time in months.

Was I relaxed from the alcohol I had consumed? The answer is no. I've tried that kind of "medication" one too many times; it only leaves a person on an emotional rollercoaster. One second, there's some joy, and the next minute, there's anger. Then, that's usually followed by revenge. Trust me, self-medication is not the answer.

This relief was brought on by the vision of my two little kids hugging me and telling me that it was going to be okay. I played it over and over in my head and then I did something that I hadn't done alone for a very long time. I got off the sofa and on bended knees, I started to pray. I said out loud how tired I was and how much pain I was in. I said that I wasn't sure how this was all going to turn out and that I was scared. As much as it felt like a relief and a breath of fresh air to let it all out, I basically was praying in a demanding tone. I wanted answers, I wanted results, and losing everything was not an option.

This went on for what felt like the entire night. I felt like I went into another universe, almost a dream state.

I don't remember where I finished my prayer or if I even said amen, and I do not remember falling asleep.

But there I stood, at the bathroom sink, with water running down my face, tired from the night before, and exhausted from a year's worth of living in the trenches, living in fear, fear of what would happen next. What would happen to my children if this would lead to a divorce, and the battles and arguments over it? I hated the fear of losing my wife, and the emptiness of the thought of being alone.

It was my two little children that forced me to look at the man in the mirror. It was there that I saw a man that lost something more. He lost his spirit. He lost his soul. I took a deep breath, and thanked God for those two little blessings that might have saved my life, and I realized, I needed to get better.

I wish I could say that at that point, I knew it was all going to be okay. I truly wish that because then this is where my story would end, and I could just write, ***and Tom lived happily ever after. The End.*** But I can't.

I will tell you that it was a huge stepping stone in my journey. Bigger and better things would be manifested from that night when I said my prayers to God. There is an old saying that I read literally days before the night at the firepit: **Let go, Let God**. Basically, it means that you have so much faith that you can let go of the past and your fears, give them to God, and just let God help you and direct you as you live for today. It sounds crazy, right?

It certainly sounded crazy to me the first day I read it. It took time and certain events for me to truly believe it, but it stuck with me nevertheless, and would be brought to light very soon.

Being human, we want questions answered immediately, and we want those answers to be exactly the answers we want. We live in a society that demands that everything happen now. Fast food is just that – order it, get it, eat it. When we are sick, we demand a pill to cure us as we walk out of the doctor's office. In my case, I basically wanted someone, something, or a Divine intervention to restore my life. Does any of this sound familiar? Maybe you have a fear that hurts so bad that it makes your skin crawl, or an anger that is so deep that you think the worst things you never could have imagined before. Or maybe you're struggling with ego, thinking it's all about you. As the next year or so progressed, there were several key moments that were life-changing experiences for me, and as I share them with you, you might relate, and they might stir up the past for you. But please HAVE FAITH. I know for a fact that there are more blessings in disguise that will triumph over the hurts and pains you are experiencing.

Yes, I'm giving away the ending. Why? Because like I wrote earlier, you are worth it. I ask that you continue to say that over and over as you read my journey: "I am worth it." We are all worth seeing the next day. And as hard as it was to face the next day, and the day after that, and the next month to the next year, I'm here today, and I'm able to share with you the joys and blessings that each day has to offer.

Of course, some days won't always run parallel with this kind of new thinking for you. I'll admit that at times, I had to fake it till I could make it. But there was no faking anything that day. I knew it wasn't going to be easy, but on that day, I dried my face, took one last look in the mirror and decided to step out of the trenches.

CHAPTER TWO

Light

"She says she talks to Angels."
~The Black Crows

At that point in my story, I did step out of the trenches...
barely. I think it was more like one foot in and one foot
out. I so wanted to be better but being separated from
my wife while still living in the same house was a huge
challenge. As hard as it was, though, I was too scared to
leave because I was too afraid of the unknown.

The one thing that didn't stop was my prayers at night.
Every night was a different prayer. Sometimes I begged
for a miracle, sometimes I just cried. Mostly I prayed for
a sign that it was going to be okay. When you are broken,
you never see the clues or signs that are all around you.
But there was one sign or miracle I did see coming, and I
wasn't sure I wanted anything to do with it.

You see, one night, I had a tough battle, and after a
heated argument about our marriage, I went back to the

renches and hid. The fear was once again overwhelming me. I tried to sleep but my mind raced. I tossed and turned till I finally jumped up, and for some reason, I decided to go check my email. As my email opened, I noticed that I had a recently sent message from a very dear friend of mine named Linda asking if I was okay. I thought, wait, what? Why is she asking if I am okay? It was like 12:30 am, and I had just spent over two hours battling with my mind, and now, my friend who knew nothing about any of this was asking me if I was okay? It was very creepy, and it sent shivers down my spine.

So, I replied to that email with a "NO, I'm not okay," and hit send. One minute later she replied, **"I'm so sorry you are going through this."** I responded with, "How the heck do you know anything is going on and how I feel?"

We went back and forth with emails that night for over an hour. I swear, she kept me sane that night. Through email conversations, she switched my mode from hate to laughter and from tears of frustration to a sense of calmness. But how did all of this come about? How was it possible that she knew I was suffering at that moment? Was it a miracle from God? Was it possible someone messaged her? Was this a prayer answered? The answers to all of those questions are yes.

Days after that happened, I was talking to her husband, a very dear friend of mine who I had worked with my entire life. To this day, I thank God for this guy. Even though I never fully opened up to him about my separation and the battle I was going through, he saw the pain every day on my face. He kept me in check and made sure I showed up for work. He pushed me to stay focused on my duties and talked to me about random things to keep my mind off of what was going on in my home life.

But this day, he told me something that blew me away. In the most serious voice, he went on to tell me that his wife has a gift. He told me it was something she had known ever since she was a child, but only recently had she accepted it. What he was telling me is that she is a psychic! Enter the crickets… dead silence.

I stood there with my mouth open, staring at him like he had three heads. "A psychic?" I replied. "Like a person that talks to the dead? Someone that can tell me my winning lottery numbers kind of psychic?" He laughed and said, "not quite." He went on to tell me that I should go talk to her and see if she could help. My first thought was, no thanks!!! That's like some kind of black magic I want nothing to do with. I didn't understand it, and I only knew what I was raised to believe, which is that psychics were the works of Satan and that they sit in little shops and steal your money.

I went home that night with all of this on my mind. My first question was, how could she help me? And that led me to the night she emailed me. I wondered if it was possible that she had "known" or "felt" that I was hurting? And why would a person I trusted for so many years want to hurt me in the long run with this "gift" she claimed to have?

So, I emailed her with questions, and she replied explaining about her gift. It was totally amazing and scary all at the same time. Question after question, I was so intrigued. But in the back of my mind, there laid a shred of doubt. If you're learning about something that is so different from what you were brought up to understand, doubt will always come up, and it's easy to disregard things that make no sense to you. Imagine if you tried to explain to someone a hundred years ago that it would be possible to wear a watch on your wrist that you could use to communicate with people in far-away places. You probably would have been chased with pitch forks.

My emails and questions to her went on for some time until finally, I decided that I would actually meet with her and put her gift to the test. I was now excited more than scared. I felt there would be no harm, and she wanted no money. I was keeping all of this to myself anyway. I emailed her about setting a date, and we agreed that the coming Saturday morning would be best. It was Wednesday, and the next three days seemed like an eternity.

That Saturday morning is imprinted in my mind forever. It was cold and snowy, and I can still smell that crisp, winter air as I got in the car and headed to Linda's house. A forty-minute drive left me with a lot of time to think about what was in store for me. I wondered if I was making the right choice by meeting with her, and I thought about what she would say and how this could help me and my situation. I remember wondering what others would say if they found out I was going to a psychic for help. My mind swirled with questions and thoughts.

One thing was for sure, I was being led by some kind of force or energy. I know this because of the way I felt the three days leading up to my visit with her. There was a difference in my attitude. I seemed not so much happier, but calmer. I slept better, which says a ton. When I would lay my head down on the sofa, I found myself breathing more easily and my heart wasn't jumping out of my chest. My mind didn't race with pure negativity, and for the first time, I caught myself thinking of getting better. I would wake up and instead of the first feeling being fear, I instead walked a little taller with some strength and courage even though I had no idea what the outcome of my life would be. So yes, I felt guided to go see Linda.

But, when I arrived and parked the car, I sat there, frozen. I tensed up and started to doubt what I was doing. I even started to cry a little because I was beginning to feel so sad about where my life had led me to that point. I looked up into the clouds and said out loud, "If I'm supposed to be here, why am I so scared to get out of the car right now?" That's when I turned my head to the house and saw Linda standing there waving her hand encouraging me to come in, so I let out a breath and decided it was time.

I knew at that moment that I wasn't scared of Linda; I only feared what she was about to say. I feared she would confirm that maybe my marriage really was over, and I trembled at the fact that God was angry at me and blamed me for where my life had led. But I needed to hear it, and we walked in together.

She saw the tears still in my eyes, so she got me some tissues and assured me that everything was going to be okay. I didn't know if she meant my life or what was about to happen next. We walked into her room where she does her readings, and she told me to sit down and relax. It's funny how at first, I couldn't even look up at her, like I didn't even know her even though I had known her for most of my life. But that ended quickly, and we began to chat.

First, she told me how sorry she was that I was going through this and that she could feel my pain. She then asked me, "What do you want, Tom?" With my hands clinched, I bluntly said, "Is my marriage over?" Linda leaned towards me and looked right into my eyes and said, "Tom, this isn't about your marriage, this is about you!"

Then she leaned back, and I could tell a switch had flipped inside of her. She wasn't talking like the Linda I knew most of my life anymore; she was speaking with the gift. No, she didn't get up and dance around the room and throw dust in the air, nor did she speak in a crazy voice like in the movies. Her head didn't snap back, and her eyes didn't roll back in her head. But her message was clear, and as my angels spoke through her, she said, "Tom, your angles want you to know that you will get though all of this. You are loved Thomas, we love you, God loves you, and people all around you love you. You must understand that. We are with you at all times. You might not feel us right now, but as you heal, loosen up, and begin to trust again, you will believe it's true. You can count on us."

With tears rolling down my face, I couldn't believe what I was hearing, and what seemed like an eternity's worth of pain trapped inside of me was exhaled out in one long-held breath.

Linda went on, "You also need to know Thomas that you have gifts as well. You are a lightworker, and you need to start using your gift to help others. Once you begin to heal, you will be able to help others heal as well. God has big plans for you. Continue your growth in faith, study, and start spreading the true love that is buried deep inside of you."

At that point, I was somewhat in shock, and a strange sense of inspiration flowed through me along with tons of questions.

How can I do all of this? I don't even know where to start. I don't know if I can heal or love again. And what the heck is a lightworker? Through Linda, the angels continued on and said, "Build your faith and your dreams, and we will help you every step along the way. God loves you as he loves all his children."

At that point, Linda seemed to slowly come back and start to talk through herself and her own words and thoughts. "Tom, you need to start being more positive today. It's your faith that got you here today! You have a lot of stuff you collected over the years that needs to be released, fears that came about way before your separation. Secondly, to understand what a lightworker is, you must study. Basically, you're going back to school!"

I asked how all of this would come about and Linda replied, "Continue your prayers, and ask for direction. You will be amazed at how things will start to pop up. A book will suddenly appear, maybe an online class, and certainly the right people will show up in your life. And remember, keep your eyes open, not everything or everyone is what you expect them to be. Sometimes, the best lessons come from the things we judge as the bad or ugly. But the biggest thing you learned today was that you are a good person and you are worthy. You made some mistakes like we all do, and God still loves and believes in you. You're going to be okay, Tom."

At that, I cried again, and I told her I was broken, which I admit was something I hadn't shared with anyone before. I was beaten and tired. It was so hard to share that with anyone because I was so afraid that I would look weak. But I was so tired of crying every single night, worrying about what my future had in store for me and my family. I shared that I couldn't imagine my life starting over, and that this was not the way I had planned it. This was the biggest hurt I had ever experienced in my life and I wasn't sure I could heal from it.

It was then that she said four little words that summed up the entire morning. "Let Go, Let God." Yes, these words that I had read once before had come back to me, and a breeze could've knocked me over. "Tom, you have to let go of the past and understand you can't change what happened. But you can change how you feel and act, and you can have love and faith from this moment on. Change is good, it's not always easy, but change is good!"

She stood up, and in a mother-like voice, she told me to get up and get moving! "You can do this, and you know God and your angels are working with you. Believe!"

I gave her a hug, wiped my eyes and got in my car. As I headed home, my mind raced with all the information that was given to me. One part of me was excited to think that I had gifts too, and yet the other side of me had me doubting everything Linda revealed.

Doubts are a part of fear. I was scared to think I could actually help anyone considering I was struggling to even help myself. I also still feared God, and I doubted God's love. But that doubt and fear would soon be brought to light with a day that I had never imagined, nor will forget.

CHAPTER THREE

Blame

*"Stop pointing fingers and placing blame
on others. Your life can change to the degree
that you accept responsibility for it."*
~Dr. Steve Maraboli

As days went by, I started to have a new outlook on my life. I felt that the words that Linda shared in the weeks before gave me a more positive sense of being. But unfortunately, the happier expression on my face and better attitude didn't always reflect the burning feelings that were still trapped inside of me. Yes, I was getting up each day with the "fake it till you make it" façade, but if I was being honest with myself, I was still only pretending, and that wasn't fair to me and everyone around me. One-minute, I was treating people super nicely, and the next minute, I was nasty. That's not living a life in faith and growth, and it's certainly not on the road to healing.

My biggest hurdle at that point was blame. I was still blaming everyone for my misery, pain, and unfortunes. I never knew at the time how bad it was or that I was even doing it. I guess I did it to take the pressure off of me because I didn't want to own the fact that any of this was my fault. I certainly didn't realize I was doing it when I prayed to God, but I was.

One day, I was coming home from work and with my head full of questions, I decided to stop by my church and talk to the pastor about my problems. What came out of that was truly a miracle and a blessing.

When I got to the church, no one was there, and the door was unlocked. This is never the case and truly either someone stepped out for a minute or the door didn't set properly when it was locked. I walked in and noticed a quiet yet eerie sense throughout the building. Normally, on days of service, it's loud with people hustling about. So, today was something many people would not experience.

I had no intention of staying, and whatever led me to the sanctuary was not my doing. It was so surreal walking into such quietness, emptiness, and peacefulness. All of a sudden, this place seemed so different, almost as if I had never been there before. I remember the sunlight entering in, the smell of the wood décor, and the unlit candles. I walked slowly towards the alter, which again, I felt drawn to do. I stood before it and thought to myself that this would be a good time to just rest and think, two things that had become impossible for me to do at home or anywhere for that matter.

I walked over to the pew, sat down, closed my eyes and just rested. It felt so good that I zoned out. I know I didn't go into a full sleep, but I was definitely in a state of deep rest, and for once, nothing was rambling in my mind. I actually felt no emotion or angst.

After what felt like hours, my eyes opened, and I thought to myself that I should probably get out of there before someone found me the next day curled up and asleep. I got up and walked back to the alter and decided to kneel down and pray before leaving, but with my head hung low and a knot in my throat, I couldn't seem to get anything out.

Quickly, my mood shifted. Instead of being grateful and thanking God for this time of peace and rest, my fists clinched and my heart starting to race. And what finally spewed out was "Why God, why are you doing this to me?" I looked up towards the alter and repeated. "Why are you doing this to me?" Then, I stood up and started to pace. I wanted to just leave and never come back, but there was something holding me there, and the time had come to get it off my chest.

This wasn't going to be question and answer time with a pastor, priest, or spiritual leader. I was going directly to the one in charge, the CEO, God himself. "Okay God, if you love me like you claim, why are you letting all of this happen. If I'm not a bad person, then why am I being punished?" The pacing continued, and my voice became louder. I tuned everything out and if anyone came into the building, I never would have known or cared.

"I try so hard to be a good man. All I ever wanted was to have a family and live a good life. Now, I'm a broken man, and I demand to know why you are doing this to me. Linda told me you love me; well, this doesn't seem like love to me! If I'm your child, why would you hurt me?"

Oh, I was angry, and I was now shouting and demanding answers. I was no longer in a quiet sanctuary, I wasn't concerned about the serenity I took in earlier. There was no peace. I was in a war, a battle like no other. But it wasn't a battle within my mind like I had experienced every night while trying to sleep. This was a full-on battle with God, and I wasn't winning. The more I yelled, the angrier I became, and the more I paced. My heart was pounding so fast and loud that I could feel it in all of my veins.

Until, I had no more.

I had no more strength, no more adrenaline left, and I completely collapsed to my knees. I gave up, and I started to cry. This was not like my normal "weeping in my pillow every night" kind of crying. I was full-blown bawling, until the life was completely sucked out of me, and I laid there defeated.

It took several minutes to compose myself and get back to the quietness of the sanctuary. Dead silence urrounded me. No lightning bolts or earthquakes were ocking the building. No candles magically lit before my eyes. No deep voice from the heavens directed me or answered any of the questions I had demanded answers o. I was alone, alone in quietness, just as it was when I irst walked in.

As I picked myself up to leave, I thought about how good it felt to have let it all out. My answers seemed to be left hanging, but I still felt a release of some sort. As I drove home, I thought about the way I acted and blamed God, and I realized I had also been blaming everyone else as well. If any answer was revealed to me that day, it was to a question that I didn't even ask: "Who's to blame?"

And the answer is this: I needed to stop blaming, and start taking responsibility for this hole that I was in. No one is responsible for my happiness but me.

Blaming others only passes the buck, which is so easy in life. "Not my fault," can be easily heard every day, from little children not getting their own way and blaming the next kid, to grown adults in the workplace blaming coworkers when something doesn't get finished on time. The same applies to God. I was mad because I didn't feel loved. I was broken because my life seemed to be falling apart. I was in the *trenches* and I wanted someone to get me out.

Trust me when I say, there is no advancement in the healing process, nor does happiness come about by blaming others for your past, your hurts, or your trials. Yes, others can help share in the healing and you happiness, but it is your responsibility to own it and take action.

Many blessings manifested from that day that wrestled with God, as you'll discover. But after that day I never again blamed God for anything that seemed bac or negative, or for the trials in my life.

My message to you is this: "You can do this. Stay positive, let go of blame, and Let Go, Let God."

CHAPTER FOUR

Judgement

"If you judge people, you have no time to love them."
~Mother Teresa

Little by little, I found myself getting off of the sofa, which was my place of supposed rest while in the trenches. I was finally in a place where I was seeking out things that could help me. I read self-help and spiritual books. I searched positive quotes every day and would write them down and read them whenever I felt they could lift me up.

I started to pray differently, and I would often talk to God when I was alone. I slowly became more grateful as I talked. I would drive in the morning and just look at the sunrise and thank God out loud for the wonderful artwork he painted for us.

It was so amazing how much better and softer I felt each day just from reading and striving to live a positive life, and finally there were many days when I knew I wasn't faking it anymore. Blame was being replaced with taking responsibility for my own issues. That is what living a positive life is all about. At least, it was a start.

Once again, I wish I could say that every day was like this, but it wasn't. I had many more bad days then good in the next year or so. But I can say that I was spending more time out of the trenches, then in them, and for once, I wasn't dwelling in the past every single day. I wanted to be better, and I wanted to dream again. I wanted to be happy, and that is saying a lot. Going from the bottom of the trench to at least wanting to better myself and making attempts is huge, and yes, I might not have seen it then, but I was healing. Many stepping stones awaited, and I had to continually remember to keep my eyes open for signs from above.

I was surprised to discover that my angels are with me and are working for me daily, just like Linda said they were. Sadly, amidst the fast-paced lives we lead, our angels and their signs often go unnoticed.

One day, a test of faith appeared out of the blue on the job site. A new laborer showed up and I was in no mood for a newbie. This guy was a pip – he talked nonstop and got on everyone's nerves. He seemed like a slacker that knew how to bullshit to get by, and I avoided him at all costs. Day after day, he seemed to just appear out of nowhere, and at the end of the day, as I got in my work truck to go home, I couldn't care less about where or how he was traveling.

He started calling me "T," which I guess was short for Tom, and finally one day, it started… He started asking people for money. Everyone denied him, including me. After all, I barely had any money myself, I worked hard for the little I had, and I needed to provide for my own family.

But one day, I finally caved. I had $15 in my wallet and I actually contemplated how much I should give him. But instead, for some reason, I just gave him all of it. I figured that for fifteen bucks, it was worth shutting him up. I handed it to him and told him I wanted it back on payday. Everyone there told me I was crazy and told me he was probably just going to blow it on cigarettes and booze. I assured them I would get it back one way or the other.

Each day that went by, it bothered the hell out of me that I knew I wasn't going to get my money back, and everyone would be right. But I noticed something else. Each day, this guy never showed up with any food or water. All of a sudden, the money didn't really matter. As he sat alone at break, I went over and asked him if he had lunch. He said "no," and that he was fine. He thanked me for the money I gave him and still promised he would pay me back.

I went home that night with an issue on my mind that trumped any of my problems that I was going through. I couldn't stop thinking about it. No matter how hard I tried, there he was. This guy drives me and everyone crazy, so why the hell do I even care? But I couldn't stop wondering, where does this guy live? Does he have a family? Is he eating at all? Normally, I judged people like him and labeled them losers, dismissing his problems and assuming that he probably brought them on himself. But this night was different; I actually cared about this guy and I wondered what I could do.

As I went through my normal routine that night and was packing my lunch for the next day, something came over me. It was clear and easy, and I acted. I packed a double lunch and took extra water. The next day, there he was, and once again, he was driving everyone nuts. As lunchtime was announced, I called him over and handed him the bag lunch I prepared the night before. He stood there at first in somewhat of a shock and then started thanking me and shaking my hand. He was so grateful and started to share with me a lot of what he was going through. I listened, and I soon realized that his problems and issues were just as bad as mine. I realized how grateful I was for the little things I did have, which would be big things for him.

This went on for weeks - I packed him a lunch, and he would share his stories. Then one day, he didn't show up. The others played it off saying he probably just quit, but the days went on, and he remained a no-show. I started asking questions, and found out that he wasn't missing, nor did he quit. He was in the hospital. It turned out that his sluggishness and lack of energy at work wasn't from being lazy, but a severe heart condition.

I asked where he was and decided that I would go visit him after work. When I got to his hospital room, he urned his head to see who it was, and with a smile, he whispered, "T." He didn't look good, and I could see the fear on his face, but he was so taken that I came to see him that he started to cry. Before I could say anything, he told me he'd been there for days, and nobody had come to see him or to find out if he was okay or whether or not he was going to live. I was shocked to say the least.

He had a rough time talking, but that wasn't stopping this guy. I told him to just get better and listen to the nurses and to not drive everyone there crazy with all of his stories and crap. We laughed, and it was time for me to head out. I grabbed his hand and told him I would pray for him. He then pulled me in and gave me the biggest hug, and whispered, "Thank you, T."

I left with tears in my eyes and I prayed as I drove home. I asked God to be with him and to help him. His heart was broken like mine, and I thanked my angels for letting this guy open my eyes. For a long time, judging others became standard, so much so that I didn't even realize I was doing it. This guy and the message that came with him allowed me to understand that if I was going to heal, I needed to be aware of how I was treating others in my life, and that judging anyone only weakens me.

For all I know, this guy was an angel as well, and he showed me that more changes were needed if I wanted to fully get out of the trenches. Everyone has a story; please tread lightly when comparing your life to theirs.

CHAPTER FIVE

Change

"Experience is a hard teacher because she gives you the test first, the lesson afterward."
~Vernon Law

As I continued to search for more books to help me spiritually and mentally, I often laughed at the fact that before this, I probably hadn't read more than the newspaper since high school. That says something right there. First of all, knowledge should never end once you are finished with your schooling, and we shouldn't think we know everything to the point where we stop taking lessons and suggestions in life. Plus, I really needed a change, and the time was now.

For years, I admit that I was stuck in my comfort zone, and that was enough. I had my family, and my career. Sure, I had stopped doing a lot of the hobbies and recreation that I did when I was younger, but it seemed to be enough. I would get up early, hustle out the door, and do the same ob I was doing since the first day I walked out of high school. After working all day in the construction field and traveling home late most of the time, I was exhausted, and I was content not doing much more.

Yes, I tended to the duties around the house and did what I thought a good husband and father was expected to do, but as far as expanding and traveling a step outside of what I assumed was my destiny, it was clear that I had set my anchor in my own personal comfort zone.

So, breaking out of my comfort zone by just reading was a major step, and I emphasize major even though I didn't realize it then. The reading helped me with the day-to-day struggles in my life. For instance, it kept me busy. You'd be surprised how much time goes by when you have your head buried in a book. It also distracted me from the battles in my mind and in my life around me.

I enjoyed reading stories written about faith and hope. Of course, I related to some of the authors, but not to others. And I learned that you never really know where your inspiration is going to come from. For instance, I found that a story of a man being captive during the Vietnam war and finding ways to survive and come home was more relatable to me and what I was going through then anything else.

Reading books about several things like angels, meditation, yoga, God, affirmations, the law of attraction, and healing mentally, physically and spiritually really opened my eyes to what other people in the world were doing, practicing, and healing. I remember always asking, "What if I could do any of these things that seemed so far out of my little world? Do I have the time and energy to truly invest in this? Can I heal?" I can also remember wondering if I would wake up an old man someday, living the same way in fears and regret, and that scared the hell out of me.

We all know the old saying, "practice makes perfect." Usually, we apply this to sports and coaching young athletes. We tell them not to only take what they learn on days of organized practice, but to also go home and practice as well so that on the day of the big game, they are ready.

I was starting to realize that I couldn't just read these helpful theories of inspiration and growth; I needed to apply them to my everyday life. But to really test the waters, I knew I had to go to another level. I really had to believe it, not just sell it. I needed to 100 percent put my faith into living a positive life no matter what I had to do to make it happen.

But at that same time, I made sure I flew under the radar. I wasn't sharing this with anyone, mostly because I was afraid of what they would think, and that way, if it all failed, no one would judge me or laugh and say, "I told you so."

What that meant was that I really had to not just believe my angels were real and that they were there for me like Linda said, but I had to trust that my angels had my back and were working hard to protect me. I had o believe God had given me spirit guides to guide me through this tough time even if I couldn't see them.

I had to look at God in a different light than I was used to and was brought up to believe. I became open to the fact that praying and repeating affirmations while meditating or doing yoga could be as helpful as praying at church or before supper and bedtime. Being positive to attract better things in my life also meant repeating affirmations like, "I am worth it" or "I am happy" and truly believing it with every cell in my body.

I became my own guinea pig, so to say. I started challenging what others did or said, and I stopped letting it interfere with my faith and my wellbeing so much. I started to pull positive and spiritual people closer to me, and I slowly detached myself from the negative ones.

Change is good. It's not always easy, but it continues to be my mantra now. Changes were happening more in those couple months than ever before in my life and they would surely continue. At this point, I was still on the fence about where my marriage would end up, but I did know that changes needed to be made for my health and growth so that I could be something better than the angry man I had become.

It's no lie that stress and anger will destroy you. Look up this fact right now and you will find plenty on the subject. I did and was astonished at the findings. I compared what I was doing in my own life to what doctors were writing lengthy papers and books about.

The findings of heart disease and suicides linked to stress is growing every day in the world. When I read this, I was ashamed to think about how my life was aligning with those stats, and I wanted change.

At the same time that I was digging into self-help books and trying to lead a positive life, I was also still living through daily battles. My body was hurting, and I was in pain daily. I was not even 40 years old, but I felt like I was one hundred years old. Besides the stiff joints and being overweight, I was constantly feeling like I had a cold, a sinus infection or some other kind of ailment. I also felt like my mind was no longer part of my body, like it was completely disconnected and being run by someone else. My negativity and angry attitude were in control more times than not. Because of this, it weakened me and left me vulnerable, and there was no room for reason.

Yes, everything I read made so much sense on paper, but in real life, it was easier said than done. I often wondered if giving my 100 percent would even be worth it, and there were many times when I wanted to quit. Days felt like years, and so many things would just pop up and inflect doubt that all my efforts to change, all the "positive thinking" and affirmations sometimes felt like a waste of time. Something kept pushing me, though. Thankfully, an unknown force seemed to inspire me.

But, just as the trenches seemed to get brighter, the next chapter of my journey would really test me when darkness seemed to overcast my life again.

CHAPTER SIX

Strength

"Life is short, and if we enjoy every moment of every day, then we will be happy no matter what happens or what changes along the way."
~Gretchen Bleiler

As the months rolled by, I felt more of a positive attitude then I had had in a long time. But one morning, as we were just starting to get the job site rolling, I received a phone call from my mom. She said, "Tommy, dad and I are at the hospital. The cancer is back, and it doesn't look good."

I so clearly remember that brief second before I spoke. I was completely frozen, and with everything going on in my life at the time, I just didn't expect to hear those words again. My dad had been diagnosed a year before with prostate cancer. He and his team of doctors and specialists acted quickly, and after surgery and follow up treatments, he had been completely clear of cancer.

Before I got that call, my mom and dad were gettin ready to fly out to visit my sister and her family. It turne out that my dad hunched over the night before in massiv pain and ended up in the hospital. After numerous tests, was clear that the cancer had returned, and it looked bad

I took a deep breath and finally replied to my mom "What do you mean Dad has cancer? The tests month earlier showed he was cancer-free!" My mom couldn answer this. She was upset and the last thing she needec was a hundred questions from me considering she hac a million of her own. I asked what hospital they were a and told her I would be there as soon as possible. Wher I arrived later that day, they had already decided to star chemotherapy since the cancer looked very aggressive.

I talked to my dad, and as much as he seemed sc strong during the first bout with the disease, I could sense this round was going to be different. He admitted to me that he was shocked, and he was visibly upset that the cancer had returned. He said he had been so confident he would never have to deal with this again. "Why Tommy, why again? It's not fair," he said as he started to cry. I told him that he wasn't alone, that he had a good team to help him, and that we would all be there for him to get through this so that he could beat this disease once again. I went on and said that he needed to stay strong and continue to fight, and it's those words that would sometime soon come back and haunt me.

The next several months were hard on my dad, as well as my mom. My dad continued to go to work while he was receiving treatments. He was a stickler for not missing work. All my life, I watched my parents battle colds and illnesses, get out of bed, and go off to their employment. That kind of dedication was instilled in me early on as my mom always would make me get out of bed and tell me that once I got to school, I would start to feel better. And she was always right. I guess my parents knew the law of attraction and the power of being positive too, and it now makes a lot more sense than it did when I was a kid who wanted a day off from school!

We tried to keep some normalcy in the family, and we would often bring the kids over to visit my dad to play catch or other outside games. He managed the best he could and if he was in pain, he wasn't showing it.

Fishing was one of the hobbies my dad had loved so much, and over the last couple years, he started to partake in it more often. I think trout fishing with my son made him the happiest. So, one night, I called my dad and told him that his grandson wanted to go fishing this coming weekend. Dad was elated and started to make a plan for which creek to start at, and he suggested that we end up at the lake that is local to us. I told him we would be at his house bright and early for coffee before heading out. Everyone was excited, and my son counted the days till the weekend. He couldn't wait to catch the big one with Pop.

But as Friday night approached us, my mom called me and told me that dad was not going to make it fishing tomorrow morning because he was not feeling well. There was a sense of disappointment, only because I really wanted the three of us to share a special day together, but if my mom was calling me to tell me that my dad was too sick to go fishing, I knew it was serious.

With a heavy heart, I told my son that Pop was not feeling well and was going to stay home and rest, and I assured him that we could still go fishing if he wanted to. He said we should go catch a big one so that we could bring it back to Pop and Nanna's house to show them. I kissed him and told him to go to sleep so that we could get up early and go catch that big one.

The next day as we headed to the lake, no sooner did I gather up all the fishing poles, tackle, food for us to eat, and my little boy's hand to start walking to our spot, when my phone started to ring. Normally, I would've left it go, but this time, I dropped all the gear and answered it. It was mom, and she was upset. As fast as we got everything out of the car to start our day, we quickly got everything back in and headed to their house. I explained to my son that Nanna needed us to come home, and I tried to keep my cool in front of him.

When we arrived, the ambulance was in front of the house, and they were already loading my dad to transport him to the hospital. I asked my mom what the heck happened? She said that he got up today and was ot making sense at all, and that he was in total confusion and asked for help.

As we all headed to the hospital, that sense that dad wasn't coming home again started to sink in.

More tests showed that the cancer had spread even more, and his entire body was now infected with the disease. It was so unbelievable how fast everything was happening. The pain my dad was experiencing was unbearable, and since the doctors all agreed that there was nothing more they could do, we had to make the decision we all feared. He was removed from the hospital that night and brought to hospice. He was quickly made comfortable and began the meds to keep as pain-free as possible.

I had one last time to talk in full conversation with my dad before he went into a drug-induced sleep. I told him that I loved him, and that it was okay to stop fighting if he was tired. He looked at me and with his last words, he said that he loved me too and that he was sorry. I smiled, and I stopped fighting back the tears and told him that there was nothing to be sorry for. A sense of strength I never had in my life came over me, and I was able to hold my dad's hand and give him the love and compassion he needed at that time. There is no way in hell I would have been able to do that before. I felt God present, I knew my dad's angels were taking care of him, and as the drugs kicked in, dad went into a sleep.

I sat with my dad by his side for several days, and as I did, I replayed our journey together. I knew he had a rough childhood, but he never talked about it, and I wondered how much that affected his life. I wished I could ask him if his dreams were fulfilled and if he had any regrets.

He served in the US Army, worked his butt off for over 40 years, made a home with my mom, and lived to see four grandchildren. He lived a good life, but he was far from perfect and made his fair share of mistakes.

At times, dad would say things out loud while he was sleeping there at hospice, but there were only little snippets that I could make out. It almost sounded and felt like he was going back in time and reliving his past, and there seemed to be a calmness on my dad's face from there on after.

I jotted down what I heard him say, and as I reread it later on, I often wondered if God was showing dad his journey and the positive things that he helped happen during his time on earth, ending any fear that he might have been experiencing.

Dad was surrounded by his family and friends over those couple days, and prayers, love and light filled that room as my mom held his hand and he went in peace.

During the days and months proceeding my dad's passing, I had plenty of time to reflect, and I was amazed at how in our family's sorrow, I was experiencing some peace too. I never once blamed God for Dad's illness or death, and I now know that was a huge stepping stone for me.

The uprising of love shared from so many friends was another blessing for my healing. My spiritual conversations with my friend, Linda, and my dear friend and pastor helped me understand that death might be the end of our physical time here on earth, but our spirit surely continues and only does good.

I also learned that our time here on earth is very short and valuable, and I knew I needed to continue to learn and make changes. I reflected on Dad's journey and compared his to mine. More mistakes and roadblocks would appear, and doors were about to shut as the months rolled on, but a door was about to open in the next chapter, and I was going to have to make a split decision to fight or flight.

CHAPTER SEVEN

Run

*"We are all of us in the gutter, but some
of us are looking at the stars."*
~The Pretenders, Message of Love

Just as Linda had revealed to me, people, books, and situations were continually appearing almost out of the blue, and I slowly realized that life was becoming one big learning experience.

My experience with God had now changed. I went from listening to people try to explain God, to living a life with God. Through my dad's illness and death, God showed me that I had a strength that I never imagined I could have. My eyes were now opened to the fact that there were people battling bigger issues than I was, and I learned that serving others can be better medicine then a doctor's prescription.

I even started taking Lay Ministry classes at my church because of all of this. I wasn't sure how it would end up or how it would benefit me, but I felt the call to help others. Again, I felt an unseen force and I listened. It was spiritual, and I liked it.

I also started to realize that not all people that were showing up in my journey lately were all "good" so to say, but they taught me good lessons nevertheless. For example, if I was around someone that was making fun of or judging another person, I normally would have jumped in and added to it. Instead, I started to step back and ask myself, "How is this benefitting me? Is this really worth it?" The answer was no, and I soon understood that I was not only hurting others but was continuing to hurt myself because of my own fears.

This holds true in families. So much of the lessons that carry on in life are passed down from generation to generation. Life lessons also include habits and the way we treat ourselves and others, and that was an eye-opening realization for me. I realized that everything I do is being taught to others, especially my children. I started to see a pattern, and then I soon realized that what I saw in my father, I was seeing in myself, and it would be carried on in my children even though some of those things I didn't want to pass on.

I wanted to cut certain habits off. I had to. I knew I could be the change. But how? I was still dealing with the hurt and fighting with the fact that a divorce could actually happen in my marriage. I was slowly seeing light out of the trenches. It was there. I could feel the warmth on my face, but I was tethered to the thought that I couldn't live outside of my home. As I cut so many strings over that time, I still had an iron-clad cable attached and there was no way to break free. I still lived in a war within myself and this warrior insisted it would get better if I stayed.

And then it happened.

One night, I totally put aside everything that I had learned about love, God, miracles, and change, and I started festering in fear. I feared a divorce and I feared losing my children. I couldn't wrap my head around not being there with them. Panic and anger once again fueled my body. I wanted change, but that cable was holding me so tight.

I wondered, "Where will I go? Where will my life end up?" So, I went to my wife and started asking her those questions, which at that time were simply unanswerable. It was the wrong time, but my ego wouldn't stop. Questions led to arguing, and I have no idea what triggered me to be so afraid and to stir up those emotions again that night, but once again, I felt alone and very scared.

My deepest fears took over and the war inside this warrior had to either "fight or flight." I just couldn't do this anymore to my wife, my children, and me. The arguing and my own personal battles within myself had to end.

As fast as all this went down, I happened to be standing next to the front door, and it was open. I stood there and stared out the door and with only jeans, a T-shirt, and an ɔld pair of sneakers on, I ran. I ran out of the house and continued down the street and never even realized it was raining. I ran so hard and had no idea where I was going. There was still no logic in my mind; all I knew was that I had to run away.

Running down the street turned into blocks and blocks that led me to a country road. My pace had now moved from a full sprint to more of a jog, a very awkward jog. Considering I hadn't run more then up and down the yard with my kids since my basketball days, I'm sure I was looking like I shouldn't be out there to anyone that passed me.

The rain started to feel good as it rolled over my face and I soon didn't notice the difference between that and sweat. At that point, it seemed symbolic, like a cleansing ritual, as though I was finally washing away so much of the past. Tears started to emerge as I continued this marathon with no finish-line in sight.

As I cried, I spoke out loud as my feet pounded the pavement. I was not speaking to God or my angels. I was almost two people that night. The happy, positive Tom was now telling the scared and negative Tom that he could do this. He was inspiring him, letting him know that if he came this far, he could surely continue in life. He reassured him that he was a good man, a good dad, and that he was loved. Over and over, it was repeated: "you are worth it, you are worth it."

As my hurts started to wash away that night, I started to think of the hurt I was putting on my family, and within a flash, my mind took me back to the church where I wrestled with God. I remembered that I had asked God if he loved me and that if I was his child, why was he letting me hurt? Step by step on the run, this scene played over and over again in my mind, and it was then that I received God's answer after all that time. His answer became a question back to me. "Tom, don't you love your two children?" I answered, "Of course." "Then you need to release them from the hurts too," he said.

I cried harder then, because I never realized the hurt they were experiencing, and it seemed like I was only running tonight from a problem, and I couldn't understand how that could help. Town blocks turned into miles until I came to a complete stop. I put my hands on my knees and breathed so hard. I coughed and hacked up spit. I was tired, yet I felt energized. I was drained, but my mind felt anew. I was prayed out, but I finally felt that God was not tapping out on me and that he never left my side. I was scared but I believed my angels were protecting me.

I stood up straight and said out loud, "Holy shit, where the hell am I?" I realized I had run at least 5 miles or more, and I had no phone to call for a pick up. So, I turned around and started walking home. That long walk inspired me to make some more changes and some tough decisions. I realized a door had opened for me, and it was ime to see what was on the other side. I had to have faith hat my family and I would be okay.

As I finally reached my home, I felt very grateful that he door was left unlocked for me, and I walked inside to ïnd everyone asleep and a calmness in the house. I took ɔff my wet clothes and changed. My legs and feet hurt ɜo bad and I knew tomorrow would probably feel worse. Ɩ laid down on the sofa and thought of two things that would take me to the next level. One was how great it felt to run and to be able to work things out in my mind while I did it. I wanted to continue with that somehow and I knew I would pursue it. And secondly, I knew I wasn't going to run from a problem any longer; I was going to run towards a solution. My family needed change. I needed change.

With those two thoughts left in my mind, I closed my eyes and enjoyed the best sleep I had had in years.

CHAPTER EIGHT

Chances

*"You never change your life until you step
out of your comfort zone, change begins
at the end of your comfort zone."*
~Roy T. Bennett

That night when I was on the run was one of the most powerful and positive experiences that has ever happened to me. So many valuable pieces of my broken life started to come back together after that experience. I felt like I could breathe a little easier, and I felt a sense of something I had been missing for a long time: inner strength. I had started to cut the strings of fear out of my life and I was taking more and more chances.

Stepping out of my comfort zone was as simple as being able to take that first little step towards something that could make a difference. So, instead of starting to run full marathons because of one night of running over 5 miles nonstop, I decided to start walking at night after work and once the kids were asleep. I broke some barriers by doing that. First, I always said I was too tired after work to do anything, and second, I always said I never had enough time to do something like that.

My walks simply consisted of strolls through our town and walking the different blocks nearby. It was nothing major, and I was not out to calculate miles and what my time was. What I did concentrate on was freeing my mind of everything that was going on in my life and just relaxing. And by doing so, it opened up free space in my mind for more positive things to enter.

Little steps out of my comfort zone led to more opportunities in my life. I started taking chances I would normally have turned down based on fear, the fear of being unexperienced, uneducated, or of not having time or energy. And then of course, there was the fear of failure.

I started by being active with my children's sports, helping out in simple ways like showing up to sell hot dogs at the stand, and that led to helping with coaching. Being active and running around with a bunch of little leaguers is not just fun, but it's a chance to watch and help the growth of a child.

Volunteering started to become a norm for me, and when it was time for someone to step up in my son's scouting adventures, there I was. I had no clue how to start a fire without matches, no true camping experience, and I didn't know how to cook over a fire. But I had faith that the right people would always be by my side and that my angels would protect me, and fortunately, we never had any hospital visits on my watch!

The biggest hurdle was yet to come, though. As I continued my Lay Ministry classes, my friend and pastor started to push me more and more to do pastoral duties, which included visiting the sick and elderly in their homes or in the hospital. Reluctantly, I would go, and the awkward start to each visit of not knowing what to say soon led to me just sitting back and listening. What I was finding was that many of these wonderful people were lonely and valued any visit from someone. Listening was all I had to do, and if it meant them repeating the same story from 1942, so be it. I was listening, I was shutting off all of my struggles and hurts, and I was taking the time to listen to theirs, and it was okay that I didn't have the answers. My visit was what they needed; it was their time to share what was on their mind at the time. It's that kind of words and smiles that make people feel worthier than anything else you can give.

It was hard, and still is, to watch anyone suffering, and those hospital visits were not always easy. I prayed a lot; it was the one thing I could give them and their family. Mostly, the suffering revealed to me that I was not alone in this world, and it forced me to stop comparing or rating my or others' pain above anyone else's.

That led to other things, from sitting in on board meetings, to helping out with youth group programs, to volunteering at fundraiser dinners. It was all learning experiences and when things seemed to get rough or when I wanted to quit, I focused on the fact that I was learning at all times from every situation. I strived to make the best of it all.

The hardest hurdle was still there: public speaking. Whether it was standing in front a big group or just five people, I was never comfortable. The old standby was that I never knew what to say. Secondly, the fears of not being educated enough to do so always weighed me down as well. But the real problem was that I stuttered when I got nervous.

Most people never knew that because I never shared it and because I never really stuttered in everyday conversations, but if I was standing alone before a group and I had to be the speaker, it would happen. And I was embarrassed every time it did. Fear and sweat would quickly shut me down, and I would find a way to quickly remove myself from the situation.

I realized that in order to be able to continue to step out of my comfort zone and continue my faith, I was not only going to have to overcome this fear, I was going to do it with passion. I wanted to do more than just get up and read from a book. I had to see myself and believe I was a speaker. I wanted inspiration in my life, and I was starting to feel like I could have the gift to inspire others. It was time to talk to Linda again.

CHAPTER NINE

Motion

*"Every great move forward in your life begins
with a leap of faith, a step in the unknown."*
~Brian Tracy

I continued on each night going for walks to clear my head instead of trying to go to sleep with everything in the world on my mind, and I started to wonder where everything was going to lead. The questions that kept coming up were:

"Will my marriage be saved from all this?"

"Do I really have gifts?"

"Will I ever truly be happy?"

Question after question, I would walk, think, and pray.

I decided to visit Linda again and see where all of this was leading. The funny thing is that it's common to think that people like Linda have all the answers, but most of the time, the answers get revealed by you. People like Linda just have a way of bringing it out of you.

And that's what makes Linda's gift so valuable and believable. You don't just walk in, sit down and she flips cards and answers what you want to hear. What she does is offer you key thoughts that have been clouded by whatever is holding you back from moving on. Not once did Linda ever tell me to just get a divorce because the marriage was over. If anything, I was always being led to improve myself for a better outcome. I guess that is what made me so comfortable listening to her talk. But I will admit, sometimes I just wished she would give me the easy way out, i.e. the answer I wanted.

Of course, it's not that easy, and I was slowly understanding that life is just one big lesson. Taking paths that not everyone is on can be scary and lonely at times. But you eventually start to bump into people that are either on that path wondering and sharing the same dream as you or you meet people that were put there to help serve, teach, and direct you along the way.

As I went to see Linda again, I was a little less apprehensive walking in. I had concerns of course of what my angels' messages could bring forth, but I was calmer and more excited than anything.

We settled in like last time, and before I could even start asking questions, Linda asked me a question. "Who's this woman I keep seeing over and over again?" I was curious. "Yes, I see a woman, kind of tall, hands on her hips, tapping her foot and she has that sort of 'why are you still not listening!!!!' expression on her face." I automatically sat back and envisioned my grandmother standing in her kitchen with her hands resting on her hips and tapping her foot when I was over for long visits as a little boy. She never had to say a word because her expression was enough for me to understand that I wasn't listening.

Linda asked again who this woman was, and just like five-year-old Tommy, I mumbled it was my grandmother who had passed about five years before. I immediately teared up and began to feel a sense of guilt, and I told Linda that I was letting her down.

Linda leaned in a little closer and said, "Oh Tom, she's not confirming failure, she's encouraging you to continue to move forward. She's sensing your doubts, and she's nudging you to listen! She knows you have gifts to give. She wants you to be happy. She loves you so much that she is here today to confirm your questions."

"But how and when can all of this happen?" I asked.

Linda shared that I was in sort of a "boot camp" in my life. I needed to continue with classes and reading, and she said that I should start writing and sharing with others about faith and inspiration. She said that opportunities would appear and that I would know when to step up and make the most of them. "You can do this Tom, and basically your grandmother wants you to listen and know that. Look how far you have come! Look at all the changes you have made. You are using the gifts you were given. Don't doubt and stop now. Trust me."

I wanted to hug my grandmother so badly just then. I could sense her presence (and I still can to this day), and whenever I have doubts and times of unhappiness, I can see her in her kitchen reminding me to listen to my heart, listen to the God of Love and follow my dreams. They don't always turn out exactly like you want them to, but sometimes, that's a blessing.

I certainly wanted more information from my reading with Linda. I wanted to know the outcome of what was going to happen in my marriage. I felt like I couldn't continue to live like this. It wasn't fair to me, my wife, or the kids.

But I guess things take time. I was scared to leave; I didn't want to be just another dad that bailed when things got bad. I was afraid of what others would say and think. But after what Linda shared, and the encouragement of my grandmother, I knew I had to stay strong, and if anything, get stronger.

I like that phrase, **Put in Motion**, and what happened next was yet another key that would unlock another door. I had to muster up more energy to get off the road I had been on for so long, a road of doubt and worry. It was time to break free of the past, live for today, and head into the future. A new path of health was waiting. There was another door to open, and I had to close the unhealthy one I was currently residing in. One step is all it took.

CHAPTER TEN

Goal

"Endurance is not the ability to bear a hard thing, but to turn it into GLORY!"
~William Barclay

Seasons were passing, and spring was now in full bloom. One Saturday morning, I awoke and made my way upstairs to the bathroom. I saw the scale laying in the corner and decided to do a weigh in. The last time I checked was at a physical at the doctor's office a year before. This time, either my eyes were not fully awake and adjusted or it was telling me that I had gained almost forty pounds! I got off the scale, took off all my clothes, and tried again. Well, that didn't help much. I looked in the mirror and realized the scale was not broken.

That was inspiration enough to get into some comfortable clothes and running shoes and go for a walk to burn some calories. The air was crisp, and things were starting to come alive outside. It was truly a beautiful morning. I decided to take a different path and ended up at our town park where there is a stadium and track. As I got near, I noticed several people had the same idea. I had never realized how many people walked or ran the track. Heck, I didn't even know it was open to the public.

As I got on the track, I pulled out my ear buds and tuned into some music. Enjoying myself and the different atmosphere, I watched several people lap me as I was walking, and I started to think about how much I hated running. Yeah, I had recently ran like five miles or so that night in the rain, but that was different – that was an escape. Now, I thought about the constant knee pains that occupied my legs for over a decade and the back and joint pain that had been embracing my body as years of construction work has taken its toll. I remember thinking about how I wished I could run free again like I did when I was a child.

My mind drifted over all the health books and magazine I had been reading, and I realized that this was yet another step I needed to take to better myself. I had been so focused on living a positive life and on my faith that I had thrown all physical improvement to the side. Yes, I was walking most nights, but I needed to step up my game.

Doubts were overcome that day as I picked up my pace on the track and went from a casual walk to a mild jog in the blink of an eye. "Oh my God, I'm actually jogging,"

I thought to myself, and I hoped no one would leave the track in case I collapsed.

One lap led to another, and soon another, and my quick math skills kicked in as I remembered that I only had to jog two more laps to make a mile! So, I set the goal, focused, jogged to the beat of the music, and I didn't collapse or end up in the hospital. I did it! I jogged a freakin' mile! I was blown away. I came across the finish line like I just ran the Boston marathon. Huffing and puffing, I came to a stop, rested with my hands on my knees, caught my breath, and then continued to walk.

As I gathered myself, I started to feel a little proud of what I just did. I'm sure the other track stars that were there that day got a good laugh at my appearance, but I really didn't care what they thought. I felt good. I was overweight, sweating, and breathing heavily, but I didn't care. I did something that day, and I got a rush doing it. It was something positive. I jogged a mile.

I walked a couple laps more and headed home. I still had a little over a mile to walk home so I had more time to think about what I just did and how good it felt. I noticed that when I was walking and jogging, I didn't think about the pain in my knees or my backaches. My mind went into another world and basically the only thought I had was about finishing the mile. I wanted more, and I was going to set a goal and reach it.

During that walk home, I made up my mind that I was going to exercise more often. The track was going to be my new home that summer and I was inspired. I focused on several goals. One was to jog or walk daily the entire summer. The second was to eat less and cut out as much sugar as possible. And there was actually a third goal, and that was to not step on the scale from Memorial Day until Labor Day. My goals were set and now I had to put them in motion.

I struggled early on with the multitasking of being a dad, having to work, the responsibilities of taking care of a home, and trying to get to the track each day, but I soon found any opportunity to get there. I realized it was easier sometimes to just drive there, and taking my clothes and running shoes with me meant I could go right after work. I also found times that I would just bring the kids with me and their bikes or scooters, but I basically preferred being alone.

My laps around the track increased weekly. I stayed focused on eating less and drinking more water. I didn't get into any crazy diets or special shakes or diet concoctions. I just kept it simple: less sugar, smaller portions, and no midnight snacks.

My jogs became a beautiful quiet time for me. I allowed nothing in my mind that was negative including my problems at home, and because of it, instead of coming home with stored up stress, I walked in softer, happier, and avoided the issues I had going on with my situation. I know that avoiding issues usually isn't the best thing, because it is true that eventually you have to face the facts. But at this point in my life, my journey, it was the best thing to do.

So many positives were being put in motion, and every day, I started to feel better and better. Where once I couldn't get to sleep at night or get off of the sofa in the morning, I was now sleeping and springing up each morning to start the day. I had more pep in my step, and my physical body was seeing the effects of the changes I had made. I had less aches and pains, and my joints and muscles seemed less tight. I won't sit here and bullshit you though. Many days, I did still hurt, and at times, I felt like giving up. But I set goals, I was nearing the end, and I pushed myself to the finish line.

Finally, Labor Day rolled around, and I got out the scale. I already knew by the way my clothes were hanging on me that I had dropped weight, but I couldn't believe my eyes when I stepped on the scale. I had dropped the entire forty pounds and more!

I was blown away. I did it. I set goals and they manifested! I walked away from the scale with a smile on my face and wondered what was next. I wanted more, and I liked it! I quickly changed and laced up my sneakers and headed out the door. I went immediately into a jog, and I felt so good and happy.

As I was jogging, I noticed that I was jogging faster then I normally did at the track. I was actually running, just like that night so long ago when I left the house in pure rage. But this time, the rage was replaced with inspiration.

My body felt light and my breaths were controlled. I had a sense of strength I hadn't felt in a long time, and it was a wonderful feeling.

As I ran that day, I started to pray. I thanked God for this new self and strength. I also shared that I was thankful that this door had opened for me. I knew that this path on my journey was something I needed to take, and I asked what was next?

After time in thought, I realized I was still running, not sprinting, but it was a nice pace. I was already at the park and headed onto the track. After I ran a couple laps, though, something came over me, and I was being led back off the track. I quickly found myself back on the street and heading in the opposite direction, a direction in which I had never taken.

I never doubted that change in direction that day, and as the track was now to my back and I was on a road that led away from town, I had no doubts, no fear, and I just kept running down that country road. It was like another breath of fresh air, exciting and new. I was surely breaking comfort zones, but would there be another road block or a miracle ahead?

CHAPTER ELEVEN

Release

"It is by going into the abyss that we recover the treasures of life. Where you stumble, there lies your treasure."
~Joseph Campbell

As you already know, life has its ups and downs. Just when you start seeing pitch after pitch coming right over the plate and you are hitting each one, all of a sudden, the Universe throws a curveball that leaves you swinging so hard you find yourself falling and laying back on the ground again.

As you can read from my story, this happened to me more than once. But this next curveball kept me out of the game for a while.

I was just starting to feel physically strong again, I was running daily, eating better, breathing, sleeping, and thinking better. I was not just feeling inspired, I was sharing it. I was beyond just reading about a healthier lifestyle; I was putting it in motion. And then one day, much of that forward motion was put on hold.

It was a normal day for me in the construction field, and I was climbing scaffolding first thing in the morning to prepare for a section of the building to get finished with brick and mortar. As I was taking each rung on the ladder safely to get to the top, I felt a twinge in my back that shot all the way down my leg. I got to the top and walked it off. After all, masonry is a tough industry it's normal to face a lot of bumps and pains each day.

I worked through the discomfort till break time, and I will be very honest, I didn't think much of it being that I had faced a heck of a lot worse. At break time, I walked over to the work truck to elevate my leg for better comfort. When it was time to get back to work, I stepped out of the truck and noticed my foot was starting to feel very strange. It almost felt like it was starting to "fall asleep" with that "pins and needles" feeling you get when it happens.

I tried to walk it off, but I noticed it was getting worse. Slowly, my foot started actually dragging as I was taking normal steps. I immediately laid down in the middle of the parking lot and tried to stretch it out, but nothing was happening. My foot was not waking up.

I managed to get to the ladder, and somehow, I climbed to the top and began to work again in high hopes that I just needed a little time to work it out and then it would wake up again. As noon approached and everyone was going down to take lunch, I stumbled over to my supervisor at the time to discuss what had happened. He could tell by the look on my face that I was concerned, and he told me to get to the hospital. Luckily it was my left foot and I was able to drive myself.

The entire time I was driving, I really thought I had a stroke or something. I was now in full panic mode and I rushed into the ER with my left leg following behind. I explained what happened and no one there seemed to consider my case as urgent as I had hoped.

After what seemed like forever, I finally got a nurse to look me over. She reassured me that I didn't have a stroke and she seemed more confused about my foot then I was, as the x-rays showed them nothing. I was now being scheduled for an MRI, a visit with a neurosurgeon, and I was fitted for a boot so that my foot wouldn't drag.

I got the boot that day, but the MRI and the doctor's visit would be in days, and that was too much to take. I wanted answers right away, and I had to get back to work. I was devasted.

I had finally gotten to a point of strength in my life, and now I was on the sideline. My mind, body and spirit were once again shot. Wasn't it bad enough that my marriage was on the rocks and I just lost my father? Why me? Why was this happening? My faith got me through so many doors, and I was closing others of the past. I felt like everything I had worked so hard physically to gain was completely destroyed, and now I had to wait around for answers.

As I finally got the results of the MRI, the neurosurgeon told me he found nothing and was to schedule another appointment in six weeks to see where I was. I was left astounded, thinking that's it? You found nothing? No advice, no treatment? Just sit and wait six weeks and wear this most uncomfortable boot? How will I work? How will I live?

I called my friend and shared with him what was going on. Without a pause, he told me I should contact Dr. Bob, who we both had been to for chiropractic care. I quickly doubted his suggestion, but he was persistent and shared that nobody else seems to care, and he does. Reluctantly, I called his office and shared my story with the desk secretary. She informed me that he was with a patient and would call me as soon as possible.

I don't think more than two minutes went by and my phone rang. It was Dr. Bob, and he quickly started asking questions. The first one was why I waited so long to reach out to him. He then told me to bring the results of the MRI and to get up to his office immediately. It was the first time that anyone seemed concerned and was eager to find a solution.

When I arrived, I was hustled in, and he reviewed my MRI. He too found nothing to support the fact that I had completely lost all movement of my foot. We sat, and he asked questions about how it happened. I could see the wheels turning in his head, and then he said something I will never forget.

"Tom, I don't know what's going on in your life or at home, but you would be surprised at how the body reacts to stress and worry. I believe you that there's problem with that foot, and I believe we can work it out. Let's go do some work on you."

I was blown away, but at the same time, I was so doubtful that I asked him if he really believed doing some adjustments on my body would actually help me. He turned around sharply and asked me if I wanted to try or would I rather put that boot on for the rest of my life. I could tell by the look on his face that he was not only serious, but passionate. He told me a lot of healing would come from myself, but I had to believe and have 100 percent faith.

He didn't do the normal adjustments that I previously experienced when coming in for back issues or "tune ups," as I called them. And one of the most significant exercises he performed was a procedure where he stretched my spine and opened my vertebras. I immediately felt a tingling sensation from my neck all the way down into my feet. When I told him this, he seemed satisfied for the time being and told me to get up. He then said he wanted to see me again in two days, and then twice a week after that. He told me to stay positive because most of the healing is within me.

As I traveled home that night, I started thinking that if I was going to heal, I had to give 100 percent in everything I did: spiritually, mentally, and physically. Here was yet another part of my journey. It didn't just end when I started to feel better, or when I ran that first mile or even when I lost 40 pounds. My journey wasn't over, and I wondered, was this a roadblock? Was there some kind of meaning behind this or even something from my past that triggered the collapse of movement in my foot?

I decided to call one of my many spiritual friends, Alex, who I was introduced to through Linda. I explained to her what had happened. As I told her the entire story, I went on to ask her why she thinks this could have happened and was it a punishment of some sort? She paused for a while and shared that it would be foolish to think that this was a punishment and reminded me that thinking thoughts of anything negative never advances us in life, especially when it comes to healing. She then said to look at this as a blessing.

"A blessing?" I shot back quickly. "Yes Tom, a blessing. Look at how many things you have faced and have learned from," she said. She then asked, "What is your foot doing when you try to walk?" "It drags," I replied. "Yes," she said, "It drags. You are trying to move forward, and something is still dragging and holding you back. Something in your life is still holding you back from healing, Tom. This is a blessing, and you need to be aware and remember all the blessings that got you to where you are today." We chatted some more, and I thanked her for all her guidance.

I took my boot off and sat on the sofa. I took a deep breath, exhaled, and began to pray. I thanked God for every single thing I could think of that I did have. I thanked him for my ability to see, hear, and talk. I thanked God for my shelter, food and clothing. I went on and on and counted my blessings out loud: my children, my mom, my friends, the doors that were opening and those that were closing. I did this over and over from the sun to the moon, until I just repeated, "I am blessed."

I exhaled and opened my eyes, and I set out another goal: I would not complain or think of my paralyzed foot as punishment, but as a blessing. Something more was to be healed inside of me, and I had to take full responsibility. Instead of my foot dragging and keeping me in the past, I had to see myself moving forward.

I started each morning by thanking God for all of my blessings. I would put the boot on for safety reasons at work, but I mentally assumed I was walking on my own. I would say affirmations quietly in my mind every chance I could, simple ones like, "I am healthy" or "my foot is strong and perfect," and "I am healed."

But the most powerful exercise I did was visualization. This is something I did all of my life, but I never fully grasped the power of using it until I started studying and understanding how people have used it to heal and prosper. Unfortunately, there is also the opposite effect, where we constantly envision all the bad, negative and diseases into our lives. I quickly realized the importance to always talk, think and envision in a positive way. There would be no room for the other. All the reading and studying would now be put into real practice, and I had to live up to my commitment of being all in, having 100 percent faith.

After two weeks of seeing Dr. Bob, I had my share of backlash from family members and friends, urging me to go get more tests and to see different doctors for more advice. I was being told that I was wasting my time and that I needed "real" help. I didn't argue with them, I just reminded myself to stay on track and not fall into the negative. They all were concerned for me and wanted me healed, and I knew they meant well.

When I walked out of Dr. Bob's office that Friday night, I could've easily given up and fallen into everyone else's thinking. After all, my foot was still dragging, and it had zero movement. I could hear in my mind everyone's doubts, but I walked in with my head high and I kept visualizing myself walking on my own.

Dr. Bob continued his normal routine, and while stretching out the vertebras, I felt a new rush of energy down my spine, my legs and into my toes. This wasn't like the previous tingle I had felt before. I told him what I was experiencing, and he asked me to sit up. He then pressed on my foot and asked if I could put any pressure

69

against his hand. I couldn't. He asked if I could move any toes, and I couldn't.

He helped me up and told me he would call me next week to see how I was doing. I shook his hand and told him I was not giving up, and he replied, "That makes two of us." I returned home and prayed, and once again I devoted it to my blessings. As I thanked God for all I that had, I ended with a simple phrase, "Let Go, Let God." I then said out loud, "Whatever needs to be let go of, I'm letting go. I'm very grateful, God, that I know you are with me, and my life is being cleansed mentally, physically, and spiritually. Amen."

Over the weekend, I decided not to wear the boot. I walked around as if everything was exactly as it should be. Yes, my foot dragged, but I didn't give it attention. I continued as if nothing ever happened and I didn't talk to anyone about it. I quickly changed the conversation if anyone asked me about it.

It was Sunday night, and I sat down to do my visualization exercises where I would visually see my foot moving and pretended to draw each letter of the alphabet in the air with my foot, A through Z.

And then it happened… I felt something.

I opened my eyes, and I saw my toe move, I could only move my big toe about an eighth of an inch, but it moved!! I smiled and couldn't contain myself. I saw it move! I could feel movement! I shouted out loud, "YES! THANK YOU!!!" over and over.

When Monday rolled along, Dr. Bob called and asked me how I was doing. I was so excited to inform him about my progress. He then said, "Tom, I was thinking about you all weekend, and what I was thinking is that if you were to tell me you had any movement at all, I know you will have a full recovery."

I couldn't believe what I had just heard. I was emotional. I mean, here is a guy who when all others gave up, he cared and had faith, and not only that, I was touched by the fact that he was thinking about me and my situation over the weekend. I thanked him, and he said that there's more work to be done on his end and mine.

I realized during this pause in health that I was letting go of fears that were truly holding me back as I tried to advance: the fear of the unknown, of being alone and of a divorce. At the same time that I was letting go, I also gained something: gratitude.

It took months for a full recovery of my foot, and nothing seemed more of a blessing then when I went out for my first run afterwards. I continue to this day using visualization, prayer, and affirmations. Not all things work out exactly the way I want them to, but I always try to choose the positive side to every situation. I consider all outcomes a blessing.

There will be more rough roads ahead in my journey as you read on. Some roads will split, and tough choices will have to be made to go right or left. Some roads will be dead ends and I will have to turn around and start over and cut my own paths.

I hope you know that by reading my journey, it's part of your path too. It was sent to you for a reason. Continue to know you are worth it. You are a blessing. Be grateful today.

CHAPTER TWELVE

Ego

"The ego mind both professes its desire for love and does everything possible to repel it, or if it gets here anyway, to sabotage it. That is why dealing with issues like control, anger, and neediness is the most important work in preparing ourselves for love."
~Marianne Williamson

At this point, my journey was going into its third year. As much as I had learned and practiced ways of bettering myself mentally, physically and spiritually, things at home just didn't get better. And after long and very difficult conversations, we both decided that it would be best for a divorce. These things are never easy, but we knew deep inside, it was needed for everyone to heal and move forward. That time of separation was long and hard on me. Living in the trenches was dark and lonely with too many sleepless nights of fear and waking up to face day after day of endless answers and battles.

And here I was, one door was closing, and I was just about ready to open another. Once again, I wish I could say that the worse was over, but I had yet to experience my worst fall yet, which would leave me on a doctor's table with a disease: the disease of EGO.

As the weeks went by, we both lawyered up and waited to see how all of it would pan out. During that time, I started to run more, and I became passionate about being in the best physical health possible. Every night and every weekend, I hit the pavement. I ran at the track, and I ran miles on country roads. I read more exercise magazines and wanted to apply more exercises into my runs. I wasn't your typical gym goer, so I didn't apply the idea of hitting weights, but I came up with my own routine.

As I ran, I would stop and do pushups. I would get back up and run a mile, then climb stadium steps at the track, and then run another mile, do more pushups and run to the playground where I could do pull ups on the kids' monkey bars. I continued changing it up every time I went out.

I didn't care what I ate, because I was a calorie-burning furnace. I had my mind so fixed on only physical exercise that it was the only thing I thought about. I wanted to not only be a warrior, but I wanted to look like one too.

Prayers fell to the wayside. I became disconnected from God, and it showed in everything I did. I even became cocky and felt like I was above everyone. I started judging others again and felt like everyone with problems just needed to exercise and "think good thoughts" like me and then all their issues would be solved. I thought I had the worst problems in the world and if I overcame them, then all you had to do was to get on my path and you would be fine.

As I went out on "runs" as I called them, I started to think more about me and less about anyone else. I fixed my mind on the fact that I was going to win when it came to the divorce. I started to listen to other people and views or experiences of divorce, and now that was in my head. Every pounding of the pavement fueled my desire to be on top, to get strong and win.

Night after night, push up after push up, and mile upon mile of me thinking about winning, I was consumed with the following thought: "Why should I lose it all?" Anger and hate returned as fast as I got rid of it. All the blessings I viewed as a learning experience were forgotten, and now a new war had entered the warrior. I became someone that my soul was not, someone that edged out love, sympathy, and any means of forgiveness. I EDGED OUT GOD.

My body was not only burning calories, but my ego was now burning the soul that I finally restored, and the fire was so strong. With so much fuel of fear being added, I finally imploded. One day, I woke up completely sore and tired. I had no appetite, and no ambition. I managed to get to work, but I started feeling sick and went home.

I went to the bathroom and tried to relieve myself. As I did, massive amounts of pain shot through my system. I then started to notice soreness around my groin area.

I could barely walk downstairs, and I felt like I had the flu or something. I curled up on the sofa and laid on my side. The soreness became inflamed, and the pain unbearable. I suffered through the night and I called in sick to work, which I had barely ever done in twenty plus years.

At that point, I couldn't even get up, and I thought that going to the bathroom again would probably kill me. The soreness became blisters and they opened. I knew this wasn't going away and I had to get help. I called my family doctor, and they told me to come in as soon as possible. I had no one to help me. I was alone, and I had to get up and drive myself. I'm not sure to this day how I actually did it, but I did. As I sat in the parking lot, I called the secretary in the doctor's office and told them I needed assistance getting in. Two nurses came out and helped me in, and I felt like at any moment, I was going to either throw up or pass out from the pain.

They got me inside and up on the table. I laid on my side because it was the only comfort I could find. The doctor finally came in, said that I had a temperature, and asked to look in my mouth. He didn't say anything more than, "Okay, that's what I thought."

I then had the embarrassment of having to slide my sweatpants down with my ass out there for the world to see. But at this point, all I cared about was for him to give me pain meds, so I could live again. After the examination of about two seconds, he turned to me and told me I had a yeast infection.

A WHAT?????

Men don't get those, do they? He was quick to answer yes, and he told me it was bad. He explained that you'd be surprised at how stress can wreak havoc on body. He then said that he wasn't sure what was going on in my life, but he bet it had to do with stress.

What? This was the second doctor that told me this!

I broke down and shared with him what was going on in my life, and he said, "Well, there you go. You need to take better care of yourself, Tom." I was now pissed because I told him how I prided myself on the top-notch fitness I engaged in.

"There's more to being healthy, Tom, then just physical exercise. You are fighting battles within and you better quit before this becomes worse." I remembered thinking how much worse could it be than this? I was furious because I thought all of my battles were finally over. I had spent over a year practicing to be a more positive person, taking classes on Faith and God, serving others, and stepping out of my comfort zone. How could I be diseased after spending so much time on healing?

I begged him for pain meds, but he left the examination room and came back with a diet plan (basically a list of "eat this, not that"). I said, "That's it???" He replied no, and that I needed to resolve my problems at home and take the stress out of my life. He advised me to stop running and take more hikes in nature, stop being so pissed off at the world and start being happy.

I told him I needed pain meds.

He replied, "The pain meds will only mask the issue. The pain might go away temporarily, but the disease will infect your body forever. I will give you pain medication, so you can sleep at night, and I will prescribe a cream to help the exterior of the infection, but the rest is up to you to clear up your insides."

He left the room to write up the prescriptions, and I was alone again. I laid there in silence, and I finally broke.

I cried.

And as I cried in pain, I realized how drained I was once again mentally, physically, and spiritually. I said out loud, "I can't do this anymore." Laying there all alone felt so cold, so empty. That's where I was, laying by myself, in pain, shivering.

Was this a view of what my life would continue to look like if I didn't change? What did I have to do, God? What must I change? How much more did I have to suffer? I said, "Please God, I can't fight like this anymore. I'm done with the war. I'm sorry I tried to do this myself, please forgive me. Help me, God."

And then the doctor came back in and helped me up. I reached out to shake his hand, and I told him how grateful I was that he was the doctor that ended up seeing me, and that he didn't just treat me like a number.

He looked at me and said, "Most people assume that whenever something is wrong with their health, a doctor can fix it immediately with drugs. I still live by the old saying, 'An apple a day keeps the doctor away.' We have to take care of ourselves in our mind, body and soul daily."

I went home, laid on the sofa and finally fell asleep. I stayed there for almost 5 days. It seemed like an eternity. But I rested, and it was needed.

CHAPTER THIRTEEN

Love

"See the bird with a leaf in her mouth, after the flood all the colors came out, It was a beautiful day, don't let it get away."
~U2, Beautiful Day

I managed to get back to work the following week, and I slowly regained my health each day. I eventually was able to start walking at night. I ate better foods, more vegetables and fruits and less processed food. I drank more water and less coffee and soft drinks.

But most importantly, as I walked, I began praying and using affirmations again. Walking led back to jogging, and each night, I devoted my "runs" to clearing my head and relaxing. I stopped listening to the music that I used to listen to, which was usually something that fueled me up and got me into "beast mode." I concentrated on each step, one after another. I eliminated goals of miles and times, and I just set out each night with the goal of feeling good.

Any time fear entered my mind with doubt, I would quickly replace it with a repeated short affirmation. For example, if I began feeling like I was a failing as a dad, I would repeat in my head, "I am a good dad and I am loved." I would repeat that over and over until the feeling of failure left my mind. If I began feeling tired or sore, I would repeat, "I am healthy, my legs are fresh, and I feel awesome." I never entertained anything negative during my walks, especially if it involved the divorce.

As darkness set in and the stars and moon would appear, I often looked up in amazement as if it was all new to me, and I would then thank my angels for being with me and keeping me safe. I envisioned them surrounding me, moving me forward safely.

I would often find designated areas in the grass where I would stop, stretch, kneel down, breath and pray. Again, I would thank God for all of my blessings. Many nights, I would weep as I did that. It was like a release valve. It felt so good just to touch the earth and feel connected. The weight of the world was slowly being lifted with every step, affirmation, and prayer. I was tuning in.

Every day, I was more and more becoming Tom and less and less of a warrior. And then it hit me one night: I was meditating while I was running! Meditation was something I had tried before, sitting quietly on the floor or on a chair, but I was never fully able to tune out and be in silence. Actually, I would normally fall asleep.

But out on my runs, I was being in active meditation. I was tuning out anything negative with physical motion and by using short affirmations and the power of prayer, I tuned into my soul.

Every day, I felt softer. I noticed my core was strong, but I walked with my shoulders relaxed and my hands were loose and not clinched. I talked less and listened more. And when I did talk, it was calmer and gentler. Worries began to wash away, and once again, I felt like I was running towards solutions and not away from problems.

One night, I went out for a run/meditation and I had a heavy heart. I knew that the following day, I was to meet with both lawyers and my wife to try to come to an agreement with the divorce. For months, it had gone nowhere.

After about two miles of running, I looked up to the sky and came to a complete stop. With my hands on my hips and catching my breath, I slowly walked down the empty street. I tuned out anything that was around me. I didn't see parked cars or houses. I felt like I was on a road like no other, like I stepped into another universe. As I walked, I asked one question…

What should I do?

And I received a message…

"You already know the answer Tom. You know what's best. Follow your heart, and practice forgiveness. If you expect forgiveness from others and especially from God, you must forgive others. YOU ARE LOVE." I stopped walking and just stood there and stared into the most amazing sky of stars. I thought back to the day I was on the doctors table when I had asked for help and forgiveness from God. I once again started to cry and shook my head in awe.

I took a deep breath, exhaled and continued on. I picked up my pace, jogged home, showered and went to sleep. It was a good sleep and I knew I was never alone anymore from that point on. I was loved, and I am love. I have peace, and I need to be peace.

As I went into the lawyer's office the next day, I pulled my lawyer to the side and told him that the fight was over.

He looked at me with a blank stare and said, "Okay, what do you want to do?" I told him that the last thing I wanted was for some judge to decide our family's fate. I wanted the best for my wife, my children, and myself. I didn't want my children to feel like they were objects being fought over. I didn't want the rest of their childhood to be memories of an angry divorce. I made too many mistakes already, and I couldn't let EGO ruin any more.

I said, "I want them to live with their mother in their house. I want to have an agreement that they can see me and be with me whenever they want. Now, go in there and make that happen."

My lawyer took a deep breath and just looked at me. I could tell he knew I was serious. He also could see my passion to make this right, and I was very blessed to have him on my side. I think maybe for a second, he de-programmed himself as a lawyer (where you have to fight until you win) and he felt my love. He knew deep inside that I wanted what was best, even if I had to give up everything, and I am so grateful he understood and respected my wishes.

You could have heard a pin drop when my lawyer sat down and explained my new demands. Neither my wife or her lawyer expected this, and of course, they agreed we would work peacefully on an agreement.

I walked out with a sense of pride, and I never for a minute felt like I lost. But as I've mentioned so many times, I had to run to a solution, not away from a problem, and I'm glad I did.

We both knew it was a long road ahead, and I will not paint a picture that it was a perfect relationship from that day until present. But I will say, we both tried hard to give our children the love they deserve, a childhood of less hate and more memories of happiness and peace.

One day, like many, however, was a challenge. I had had a rough couple of days fearing the future. As strong as I was, again, I'm just human, and we all have our moments. This time on the drive home, I started to tear up. That happened quite often actually, but this was different. I just couldn't wrap my head around the fact that someday, it was all going to be okay. I thought about my little kids, and how much I loved them. My thoughts of my failures overpowered any thoughts of the good I had done. I clinched the wheel and just kept crying.

I was on a long stretch of highway and it seemed like forever, and then I noticed something out of the corner of my left eye. When I turned to see what it was, there, flying alongside of my jeep was a bald eagle. Yes, a majestic, full adult, bald eagle!

I know I only looked for a couple of seconds before returning my eyes to the road, but I could see every detail in his face. His serious eyes, and his long yellow beak gave him the look of bravery. He flew with inspiration and determination and a knowing of where he was going on his journey.

When I looked back, he was still with me, flying at a perfect pace. And then, as fast as he came into my presence, he flew upward and away out of sight.

I took a deep breath and exhaled. I knew immediately that it was a sign and a message. The way he flew with such confidence and a knowing of where he was heading was exactly what I needed to understand. I needed to do the same. I was on the right path, and I had to be brave. Faith got me there, and faith would carry me into tomorrow.

With my head raised higher, I smiled, and I said thank you.

Thank you, God.

CHAPTER FOURTEEN

Worthy

"With everything that has happened to you, you can either feel sorry for yourself or treat what has happened as a gift. Everything is either an opportunity to grow or an obstacle to keep you from growing. You get to choose."
~Wayne Dyer

Those immortal words that were said to me what seems like ages ago are now my mantra: "Change is good. It's not always easy, but change is good." I now know with certainty that if anything good and full of love is to come, and for continued blessings to manifest, I must accept that change must happen. I have to continue on a road most people avoid, and I need to stay off easy street.

Yes, my faith is strong, but I would be a liar if I just finished this story with the idea that I became some spiritual guru and walked the earth without worry, able to solve all of my problems instantly.

Fat chance, and yes, it sounds perfect for a Hollywood movie, but I truly believe that kind of earthly life hardly exists. I stayed the course and I kept running. Those nights of running were more than just sweat and miles; they became keys to open doors I never thought existed. As I ran and meditated, one thought repeated itself nightly. It was the words that my angels shared through Linda, that I was a Lightworker and that I could help others heal once I began to heal.

As I ran every mile along my nightly path, I started a new affirmation, one of my all-time favorite scriptures: "I can do all things through Christ who strengthens me." I repeated that over and over and then I asked many questions concerning all of this. "What can I do next?" And "Will any of this make me happy? Will any of it help me move on?"

I was amazed and yet surprised at some of the messages I received and downloaded while meditating. I followed through with many of those messages, including...

o I started a Saturday night inspirational service once a month with live music, and I personally wrote and delivered a positive message at each one. Many of those messages were thought up or started while I was running, and yes, I sometimes still stutter, but I've learned that I'm okay with it and not ashamed.

- I wrote inspirational morning messages and sent them via email to a group of friends.
- I started running charitable 5K's and obstacle races, and I walked 24 hours non-stop to raise money for cancer research.
- I stepped up into more leadership rolls and public speaking opportunities.
- I baptized babies and even assisted in wedding ceremonies.
- I followed through with career changes that seemed impossible.

None of this would have happened if I had just stayed in my comfort zone. I would have ignored any thought of such things. Running and meditating opened my mind to possibilities. And as I got physically stronger, so did my faith, which pushed me over the bar to make things happen. I released a lot of my past and fears. I replaced judgement and blame with forgiveness and gratitude, and I now have a relationship with God. What I wanted to see in the world, I had to see in myself first.

Things were moving and changing. The divorce was seconds away from wrapping up legally. Yes, I was torn thinking about my kids, and I wondered at times if I would truly be happy again. Things that I normally would call HARD, I now have to see through a different set of eyes. But it's not easy especially if your eyes are clouded.

Yes, I know its EGO, but I'm human. And one of the best quotes to relate this to is:

"We are not human beings having a spiritual experience. We are spiritual beings having a human experience."
~Pierre Teilhard de Chardin

Between EGO, the loss of my father and the toll it took on our family, and the fact that very soon a rubber-stamped piece of paper with a judge's name on it would officially tell me I was no longer married, it all weighed on my shoulders. Plus, with Thanksgiving approaching, I knew it would be the first without my children, and that was tough.

I set out for a normal nightly run and stopped at my usual patch of grass, kneeled down and began to pray. I thanked God for getting me to where I was and for saving me. I was grateful for the blessings I had been given. I shared with God that I was blessed that he sent me angels to give me messages, and I was thankful for Linda who opened that door of communication.

And then, it was like a movie in my head; I began to review my life from my childhood to present day. It was a sobering moment as I viewed a lot of mistakes and hurts. Some were brought to me, and some I inflicted on myself and others.

But as fast as I viewed them, many good things were shown to me, and the blessings outweighed what we call failures. Strength was more present then I actually though when I was down and in the trenches. So much love and compassion were given to me from family members and close friends that opened their homes and offered an ear to listen and a shoulder when I needed to cry. There are friends that are still with me today and some that had to move on, but I will always hold them dear in my heart for the love they gave me.

When I was finished, I got up and resumed running. As I looked into the stars, I said to myself, "Well, if I'm going to be happy, it's going to be up to me."

I meditated as I ran, and then I stopped in my tracks with a thought in my head: Thanksgiving. It's supposed to be a day to give thanks, and also to give. And giving was exactly what I wanted to do.

After my father passed away at the Hospice, I made a promise to the staff that I would repay them for everything they had done for my dad and my family. If you have ever experienced a visit at a hospice, you would agree, they are what we call Earth Angels.

So being I had no plans that year for the holiday and knowing that many of the staff would not be spending time with their families, I decided that I was going to make an entire Thanksgiving feast for them: turkey, stuffing, mashed potatoes, veggies, cranberry sauce – the whole works. All of this was revealed to me from my meditation run.

On the morning of Thanksgiving, I got up at 4:00 am, and by noon, I had the feast complete and ready to deliver. During the drive, I couldn't contain myself. The happiness of doing this filled my soul. Yes, it did come with memories of my dad, and I knew it would have been exactly what he would have wanted me to be doing that day. And to really fulfill what my dad would want, I would do it without question and without revealing who or why it was done.

I did call them ahead of time to let them know they would have a full dinner that day, but I never said from whom. So, as I walked into the office area, I said I had the dinner delivery and asked where to put it. The woman behind the desk showed me where the faculty room was, and I set it all up.

As I walked out, I never said a word and I hoped I could sneak out without anyone asking me, but as I was near the exit, I heard a voice yell out… "Hey!!! Who are you???"

Without hesitation, I smiled and said, "Santa Claus!"

I walked out, drove home and being that it was one of the most beautiful and warmest Thanksgivings in a long time, I decided to change into my running clothes and hit the pavement. As I started, I thought it would be really awesome if I could run all the way to one of our local spots that we call Lake Minsi, which is about 7 miles each way. It was fitting being it was the lake that my son and dad fished at.

The furthest I had probably managed to run up until that point was about ten miles at a time, so the idea of a fourteen-mile hike was intriguing, and I knew I had the rest of the day to do it. I figured worse case, I would tank out on my way back and just call and hope somebody would come get me.

As I ran, I thought about how good it felt knowing I did something for someone else. It actually made me feel lighter as I ran. Giving replaced wanting that day. I wanted to be with my kids, and that was expected. I knew they were safe and enjoying being with their mom's family, and I accepted that.

The further I ran, the clearer I began to see things in my mind, and the biggest message to date was presented to me. It was simple…

Love.

Love is happiness. Love is the emotion I must choose to use from here on out to get through whatever faces me while on this earthly visit. I then recalled a quote from Elisabeth Kubler Ros:

"There are only two emotions: Love and fear…
from love flows happiness, contentment,
peace, and joy. From fear comes anger, hate,
anxiety and guilt. It's true there are only
two primary emotions, love and fear."

Love is not just about sex, and it's not just something you say to someone. It's real, and it's a positive force that needs to flow to keep things moving. Anything in fear eventually just stops, keeps things in chaos, and never allows us to move forward. True love, on the other hand, allows us to change, even if it seems impossible.

I knew I was getting closer to the lake, and I was getting excited to reach it. I blanked out the entire run and hardly noticed anything as I was in such a wonderful train of thought. As I made the last turn in the road and spotted the lake, I hopped on a trail path and started slowing down my pace. As I controlled my breathing, I slowed even more and walked right up to the lake. I closed my eyes and thanked God out loud. Over and over, I just said thank you.

As I opened my eyes, I was amazed at what I saw. Everything I looked at was crystal clear: the vivid colors of the fall trees, the mountain, and the sky mirroring the lake to the point that I couldn't tell which was real or which was the water making the reflection. The cloudy vision I had had for a long time was now completely clear. There was no haze and not one cloud to be found.

I let out the biggest exhale and breathed in the best breath of fresh air that I had been needing in a long time. It was then that I truly felt alive. This road led to a place my soul had been missing: Peace. It was exactly at that moment when everything was so clear that I knew the war had finally been taken out of the warrior.

I had no more use for fear in my life. Fear is the opposite of love. Hate, blame, anxiety and guilt could no longer riddle my course of travel. That meant that no matter what was thrown at me to trip me as I walk this path, I can't turn around or jump on another path where everyone else is headed. I needed to continue to pave a way through the fear and out of the comfort zone.

I found happiness, and it wasn't a place, a person, or a thing. It was the happiness of freedom to live and move on with my life; the happiness of peeling off the layers that the warrior in me had gathered and heaved in mind, body and soul.

The fear of the past and future was not an issue anymore. The happiness now laid in living in the now, and I finally understood how important that really is. Finally, happiness is something in me, and it's something I can share and not expect from others.

With the biggest smile on my face, I knew I better get back on the trail. My legs were already tightening up, and I knew it wasn't going to be easy to run another seven plus miles back. But that's how life sometimes is – it's only as easy or hard as you make it, and you can't give up.

I'm blessed that I didn't give up. I'm experiencing things I never imagined. Through a lot of time and patience, it all worked out. I eventually moved out and I stayed on the course, the road less traveled, and I'm happy I did. We did what most divorces normally can't do. My ex and I still have a decent relationship where we can talk and make decisions about the kids, and we have been able to be there for them for sports events and school functions. Why? Because of love. No, we don't love each other like husband and wife. But it's a love for our kids that made a difference. She's a great mom, and I love her for all she has done for them.

That's the meaning of happiness. That's the reason not to quit. Of course, shit still pops up, and roadblocks happen. That's life folks. But it's your attitude that allows you to see through it. Positive is always stronger then negative. Love defeats fear every time. It's when your vision is clear that you can see it.

This story was not about a divorce and never was. Linda clarified that from day one. It was about me. Yes, going through a divorce is hard. I would never entertain that it is easy, and many hurts and pains were there daily, not just for me, but for the entire family. But my fears already existed, and it was the separation period that sparked the fire.

We all have a story, and we are all on different roads. We all experience something throughout our lives that might seem to be the end. But what is true is that the end as we know it is just another starting point. We all have fires that burn in us that hold us back from moving on. Sometimes, it's the loss of a loved one or even a dissolved friendship, a loss of a job, or dreams put on hold because of the fear of stepping out of our comfort zones. The list goes on and on and so do the excuses.

As I ran home, I repeated many affirmations to get my butt back there. "You are worth it" got me through, and it is still as important today as it was then.

I am worth it, and so are you.

I send you Love, and All Good News.

ACKNOWLEDGEMENTS

I would like to thank my family and friends who never gave up on me and always reminded me that I am worthy; my friend, Linda, who opened my eyes to see the miracles in front of me; my editor and friend, Faith, for her support and hard work to make all of this possible; Mark Fiorentino for the cover photo, Shawn Stewart for the head shot, and my living-the-dream partner, my strength, my love, Carla.

CPSIA information can be obtained
at www.ICGtesting.com
Printed in the USA
FSHW012157190219
55801FS